Against All Odds: A Journey of Survival

Hama Hassan

"From the ashes of tragedy, I rose not as a victim, but as a warrior. Each battle carved my spirit, and every tear forged my path. I refuse to be defined by my scars; instead, I will illuminate the world with my triumph."

Hama Hassan

A Kurdish Citizen Story

Against All Odds: A Journey of Survival

"In the depths of despair, I found my strength; in the shadows of loss, I discovered my light. Every scar tells a story, and every struggle is a step toward the life I dare to dream."

To my beloved brothers, friends, and cherished family,

In the tapestry of my life, each of you is a vibrant thread woven with love, strength, and unwavering support. Through the storms that have tested us, you stood as my pillars, offering hope when darkness loomed and laughter when despair threatened to consume me.

To my brothers, you are not just my family; you are my heart and my resolve. Together, we have navigated the depths of grief and emerged stronger, carrying the weight of our dreams on our shoulders. Your courage inspires me daily.

To my friends and relatives, your kindness and loyalty have been a beacon in my journey. You remind me that even in the hardest of times, we are never truly alone. Thank you for being the light in my life, for the shared memories that bring joy, and for the countless moments of understanding and compassion.

Together, we have built a bond that transcends the trials we face, and I am eternally grateful for each of you. As we continue this journey, may we always find strength in each other and embrace the love that binds us.

With all my love,

Hama

Contents

Preface

Life is a tapestry woven with threads of joy, sorrow, resilience, and hope. My journey, marked by the beauty of childhood and the devastation of loss, reflects the complexities of existence. Born in Iraq in 1994, I was blessed with a childhood filled with laughter and love, supported by a devoted family who nurtured my dreams. However, the shadows of conflict soon crept in, forever altering the course of my life.

This book is not merely a recounting of events; it is an exploration of the human spirit's capacity to endure in the face of overwhelming adversity. The loss of my parents and uncle during a time of chaos shattered my world, but it also ignited a fire within me—a determination to rise, to rebuild, and to honor their memory by forging a path toward a brighter future.

As I share my story, I invite you to walk alongside me through the valleys of despair and the peaks of triumph. You will find moments of heartbreak, resilience, and the unyielding love of family and friends who stood by me when I needed them most. This narrative is a testament to the strength of the human spirit, the bonds of brotherhood, and the relentless pursuit of hope.

Throughout my journey, I have learned invaluable lessons about perseverance, the importance of community, and the necessity of believing in oneself, even when the world feels heavy with despair. It is my hope that by sharing my experiences, I can inspire others facing their own struggles to find strength within, to seek support from those they love, and to never lose sight of the light that can guide them through the darkest of times.

Thank you for joining me on this journey. May we all find the courage to embrace our stories, to seek our dreams, and to cherish the moments that make life worth living.

With gratitude,

Hama Hassan

Against All Odds: A Journey of Survival

Prologue: A Life of Struggles and Triumphs

Life, as I have known it, has been an unpredictable journey—a blend of joy, pain, hope, and perseverance. Born into a family filled with love and privilege, I never imagined that tragedy would strike at the heart of my existence. My early years were bathed in warmth, surrounded by the comfort of my parents and three brothers. Our family was blessed; we were rich, not just financially, but in love, security, and the simplicity of childhood happiness.

But then, the world changed. The invasion of Iraq in 2003 marked the beginning of a new chapter—one that would tear my family apart and alter the course of my life forever. I was only ten years old when I first encountered the horror of war. The constant fear of death and loss became my reality. And then, the unthinkable happened. In 2005, I lost my parents and my uncle in a tragic accident that would define my future. In a single moment, my childhood was stripped away, and I was left to face a world that no longer felt safe.

Despite the overwhelming grief, life had to go on. As the eldest, I had to step into a role I was not prepared for—becoming the pillar for my brothers. We moved, we adapted, and we tried to rebuild our lives in a world that no longer made sense. Education became my solace, and I pushed forward, earning a degree in petroleum engineering. But even then, the road to success was fraught with challenges.

After countless rejections, a surprising opportunity came in the form of a job as a tax accountant for a UK-based company. It was far from the engineering career I had envisioned, but it was a lifeline. It allowed me to support my family and myself, providing stability in a time when stability seemed like a distant dream.

Through it all, I have learned that life is unpredictable. It will test you in ways you cannot imagine. But it will also reward you with moments of beauty, friendship, and the kind of love that sustains you through the darkest times. My journey has been one of survival, of rising from the ashes of loss and despair to find meaning in the everyday moments of life.

This is my story—one of struggles, triumphs, and an unrelenting hope for a better tomorrow.

Part 1: The Early Years

Chapter 1: A Blessed Childhood

Birth in Iraq (1994)

In 1994, Iraq was a country caught in the grip of political tension and economic sanctions. Yet, for me, this world began in a cocoon of love and security. I was born in Baghdad, the capital city of Iraq—a place once known for its rich history, culture, and intellectual legacy but, by the time of my birth, already plagued by instability and the looming shadow of war. Nevertheless, to me, Baghdad was simply home.

My birth was a celebration for my family, a family steeped in both tradition and ambition. I was the first child, a son, born to parents who showered me with affection, hope, and dreams for the future. In those early years, the external chaos of the world was far from my understanding. I only knew love, care, and a deep sense of belonging.

Family Life: Father as Head of Engineering, Mother as a Housewife

My father was a man of exceptional intellect and ambition. As the Head of Engineering in Iraq, he had earned the respect and admiration of his peers and colleagues. His work involved overseeing large infrastructure projects, dealing with complex technical challenges, and contributing to the modernization of Iraq in the midst of its turbulent times. Though he was a busy man, always caught up in the demands of his career, he made sure to carve out time for our family. He was not just an authoritative figure but a guiding light in our lives. I remember him as a calm, composed, and wise man—someone who was always willing to impart lessons of life, science, and hard work.

My mother, on the other hand, was the heart of our household. A housewife by choice, she devoted her time and energy to raising me and my three younger brothers. She was the embodiment of warmth and care, creating a loving environment where we were nurtured both physically and emotionally. Despite the fact that our family was quite affluent, my mother never allowed material wealth to overshadow the values she instilled in us: humility, kindness, and respect for others. She kept our home running like a well-oiled machine, ensuring that we were fed, clothed, and loved unconditionally.

The balance between my father's professional achievements and my mother's unwavering dedication to the home made our family a stable unit, a fortress where we felt protected from the outside world. My parents were a perfect team, and their partnership created a sense of normalcy and harmony that I would come to miss dearly in the years to follow.

Life in a Multi-Generational Home with Grandparents and Uncles

Our family lived in a large, sprawling house that belonged to my grandfather. It was not just a house but a multi-generational home, where I grew up surrounded by my grandparents, uncles, aunts, and cousins. We occupied the upper floor, while my uncles and their families lived on the second floor, and my grandfather, the patriarch of the family, resided on the ground floor. It was a lively, bustling household, full of love, laughter, and the occasional quarrels that come with living in such close quarters with extended family members.

The presence of my grandparents added a layer of wisdom and tradition to my upbringing. My grandfather, a man of few words but great knowledge, would often sit on the porch in the evenings, sharing stories of the old Iraq—a land rich in culture and history. His tales of the past fascinated me, filling my young mind with wonder about the country I was born into. My grandmother, on the other hand, was the epitome of patience and kindness. She was always in the kitchen, preparing elaborate meals for the entire family, and her cooking became one of the most vivid memories of my childhood. The scent of spices, fresh bread, and slow-cooked meats would waft through the house, creating an atmosphere of comfort and togetherness.

Living in a multi-generational household meant that I was constantly surrounded by people who cared for me. There was never a moment when I felt alone. Whether it was playing with my cousins in the yard, listening to my uncles talk about politics and work, or sitting by my grandparents as they shared their wisdom, I was always enveloped in the warmth of family. It was a bustling life, filled with activity and shared experiences. We would gather for meals together, often at a long dining table, where everyone's voice blended into a symphony of chatter, laughter, and occasional debates.

My father's brothers were also a significant part of my early life. One of my uncles was a doctor, a respected man in the community who had a passion for helping others. His stories of treating patients, even in the most challenging circumstances, filled me with admiration for the profession. My other uncle worked in trade, often traveling to other regions of Iraq to conduct business. Both of them, in their own ways, were role models to me, showing me that success could be achieved through hard work, education, and dedication. I was lucky to be surrounded by strong male figures who not only provided for the family but also stood as examples of integrity and perseverance.

The house itself was a place of childhood wonder. It had wide hallways, tall ceilings, and a garden where I would spend hours playing. My brothers and I had the third floor all to ourselves—a space filled with toys, books, and our imaginations. We often played soccer in the yard or rode our bicycles in the neighborhood. The sense of security that came from living in such a close-knit family unit was unparalleled. In those early years, the world seemed like a place full of endless possibilities, and I was blissfully unaware of the hardships that lay ahead.

Early Friendships and Childhood Activities

My childhood was not just shaped by family but also by the friendships I made during those early years. I grew up in a neighborhood filled with children my age, and we formed a close-knit group that spent nearly every day together. My friends Karim, Steven, Ali Zita, Omar, and Fadi were like brothers to me. We were inseparable, spending long afternoons playing soccer, riding bicycles, and watching cartoons together.

Our favorite pastime was soccer. We would play for hours, often turning a dusty patch of land near my house into our makeshift field. Our games were intense, filled with the kind of passion that only children possess. We would argue over goals, celebrate victories, and laugh at our own mistakes. Those matches were more than just games—they were a bonding experience, teaching us about teamwork, competition, and the joy of simply being together.

When we weren't outside, we would gather in my house to watch cartoons and movies. My father had a collection of VHS tapes, and we would sit in front of the television, mesmerized by the adventures unfolding on the screen. It was during these moments that my love for the English language began to grow. Watching movies in English, often with subtitles, helped me pick up new words and phrases. My father would sit with me sometimes, translating the dialogues and explaining the context, making sure that I understood the stories. Little did I know that this early exposure to English would later become one of my strongest assets.

Apart from soccer and cartoons, our group of friends also loved exploring. We would venture out into the neighborhood, often riding our bicycles to new places, pretending to be adventurers on a quest. The world felt so big back then, and every corner of the neighborhood seemed like a new discovery waiting to be made. Sometimes, we would end up at the local market, where we would buy candy or snacks with whatever little money we had. Other times, we would visit each other's houses, where our mothers would treat us to homemade sweets and drinks. It was a simple life, but it was full of joy and innocence.

In those early years, the world felt like a safe place. My family was whole, my friendships were strong, and my future seemed bright. I was too young to understand the political turmoil brewing around me, the economic hardships my country was facing, or the impending war that would soon shatter this idyllic existence. For now, life was good, and I cherished every moment of it.

In hindsight, my early years were a golden period—a time when I felt loved, safe, and happy. I was surrounded by people who cared for me deeply, and I had the freedom to explore the world with wide-eyed wonder. These years laid the foundation of who I am today, giving me the strength to face the challenges that were yet to come. Little did I know that this blessed childhood was only the beginning of a much more difficult journey—one that would test every ounce of my resilience and redefine the meaning of family, love, and survival.

Chapter 2: The War Strikes

The Invasion of Iraq (2003)

By the time 2003 arrived, the world I had known in my early years began to crumble. The Iraqi capital, Baghdad, was suddenly thrust into chaos as the United States and its coalition forces launched a full-scale invasion of Iraq. I was nine years old when it all began. The war that had once been a distant subject of conversation among adults was now our brutal reality. The invasion came under the pretext of disarming Iraq of weapons of mass destruction, but for the ordinary citizens living in the crossfire, the reasons seemed irrelevant. The only thing that mattered was survival.

As the bombing campaigns started, our quiet neighborhood was no longer safe. We could hear the distant hum of jets overhead, followed by deafening explosions. The nights were the worst. Darkness provided no comfort, only more fear, as the sky lit up with tracer fire and rockets. The ground shook with every explosion, making the walls of our multi-generational home tremble. We huddled together, my brothers and I clinging to my mother while my father and uncles tried to stay calm. They reassured us, telling us the war would pass, that we would be safe. But deep down, I could sense their worry. The invasion had thrown everything into uncertainty.

Electricity became a luxury, and with the collapse of infrastructure, the once-bustling markets now stood desolate. Schools were closed, and life, as we knew it, was put on hold indefinitely. Our days were spent indoors, with little to do but pray for the war to end. My father still went to work as much as possible, trying to maintain some semblance of normalcy, but even he could not escape the toll that war was beginning to take on all of us.

Rising Dangers for Kurds, Christians, and Minorities

As the war intensified, a new kind of danger began to emerge—one that targeted specific ethnic and religious groups within Iraq. My family, being Kurdish and Christian, was part of two minority groups that suddenly found themselves at even greater risk. Under Saddam Hussein's regime, Kurds had long faced persecution, but the removal of the government in 2003 led to a new power vacuum that unleashed chaos. Various militant groups and factions, emboldened by the disarray, began to assert control over different parts of the country.

The danger for Christians and other religious minorities was also increasing. Iraq had always been a religiously diverse nation, but the war created a breeding ground for extremism. Christians, seen by some as allies of the West because of their shared faith, became easy targets. There were reports of kidnappings, bombings of churches, and forced conversions. My family, being both Kurdish and Christian, suddenly became more vulnerable than ever. My father and uncles began speaking in hushed tones, strategizing about how we could stay safe in the midst of this rising threat.

The once-peaceful streets of Baghdad became perilous, not just because of the ongoing war but because of the random acts of violence that erupted everywhere. Car bombings, shootings, and kidnappings became part of daily life. Fear became our constant companion, and we could no longer trust anyone outside the family. Even the simplest of tasks—going to the market or visiting a friend—became fraught with danger. The war had not only brought destruction but had also torn apart the social fabric of Iraq. Communities that had lived together in peace for generations were now divided by sectarian violence.

First Brush with Danger: The Shooting in 2004

By 2004, the war had seeped into every aspect of our lives. Baghdad was no longer the vibrant city I had known in my childhood. It was a war zone. The U.S. forces were now entrenched in the city, and insurgents launched attacks daily. Roads were blocked, checkpoints were everywhere, and danger lurked around every corner. It was during this time that I had my first real brush with the violence of war.

One afternoon, my father and I were out running an errand. We needed to pick up some groceries, something that had become an increasingly difficult task as the city descended further into chaos. We were walking back from the market, bags in hand, when suddenly gunfire erupted nearby. I remember the sound distinctly—it was sharp and terrifying, nothing like the fireworks I had once enjoyed watching as a child. My father grabbed my hand and pulled me behind a nearby wall. We crouched down, my heart pounding in my chest as the gunfire continued.

I could hear people shouting and the unmistakable sound of bullets hitting metal and walls. My father held me close, his body shielding mine. We waited there for what felt like hours but was probably only minutes. Eventually, the gunfire subsided, and my father peeked around the corner to check if it was safe. When we finally made our way back home, my father's face was ashen, his usual calm demeanor replaced by a look of grim determination. That day marked the first time I realized just how close death could be in a war zone.

Life-Altering Tragedy: The Loss of Parents and Uncle in a Car Crash (2005)

The year 2005 brought with it the most devastating event of my life—a tragedy that would alter the course of my future forever. It was a typical afternoon, much like any other in those years of war, when my parents and my uncle went out to attend a family gathering in another part of the city. My brothers and I stayed home, safe in the comfort of our multi-generational house, awaiting their return. But that return would never come.

Later that evening, we received the news that my parents and uncle had been involved in a horrific car crash. Their vehicle had collided with another at an intersection, a moment of chaos in a city already unraveling from violence. The impact was devastating, and none of them survived. I remember the moment I was told— time seemed to stand still. My world, which had already been shaken by the war, crumbled entirely.

In an instant, I was an orphan. The loving, protective world that my parents had built for me was gone, wiped away in a single, cruel moment. My father, the steady, wise figure I had looked up to, and my mother, the kind-hearted woman who had nurtured me and my brothers, were both gone. My uncle, too, who had been such a significant part of our lives, was lost.

The grief that followed was indescribable. I remember feeling numb, as if I had been hollowed out from the inside. The house that had once been filled with laughter and love now felt empty, haunted by the absence of those we had lost. My brothers and I were devastated. We clung to each other, but no amount of comfort could fill the void left by our parents' deaths. The extended family, though still supportive, could not ease the overwhelming pain.

This tragedy, compounded by the ongoing war, forced me to grow up quickly. At the age of eleven, I found myself having to navigate a world without the two people who had shaped me the most. The loss of my parents marked the end of my childhood. The war had taken so much from us already, but the loss of my parents was the most profound blow. It was a turning point—a moment when I realized that life would never be the same again.

In the days and months that followed, I tried to make sense of the senselessness of it all. The war had taken so much from us already, and now it had robbed me of the two people I loved the most. But as hard as it was to cope with the grief, I knew I had to keep going. My parents had always taught me the value of resilience, of pushing through hardships, no matter how difficult. It was their legacy, and I was determined to honor it, even in the face of this unimaginable loss.

The loss of my parents and uncle in 2005 became the defining moment of my life. It marked the end of the innocence of my early years and thrust me into a world where survival was no longer just about avoiding bombs and bullets but also about finding the strength to carry on without the people I loved most. In the years that followed, I would draw on the lessons they had taught me—their values, their love, their resilience—to navigate the darkest times of my life. But in those early days of grief, all I could feel was the immense weight of loss and the uncertainty of a future without them.

Chapter 3: The Aftermath of Grief

The Trauma of Witnessing the Deaths of Loved Ones

In the days following the loss of my parents and uncle, the world felt like a dream—a nightmare I couldn't wake up from. The trauma of losing them in such a sudden, violent way left an indelible scar on my soul. Even though I hadn't been there to witness the accident itself, the weight of their deaths bore down on me, gnawing at my mind. I had replayed the moments leading up to their departure over and over, thinking about what I could have said, or what I should have done. Perhaps if I had begged them to stay home, they wouldn't have gone out that day.

I couldn't escape the images my mind created—vivid, haunting visions of the crash. It was as if I had been there, seeing the twisted metal, the broken glass, the lifeless bodies of my parents and uncle. My thoughts spiraled into guilt, even though I had no control over the events that had unfolded. But grief plays cruel tricks on the mind. I felt helpless, unable to protect the people I loved the most. I began having nightmares, waking in the middle of the night drenched in sweat, my heart pounding as if it had been me in the wreckage.

My grief wasn't only emotional. It manifested physically, too. Some days, the sadness was so overwhelming that I couldn't eat, sleep, or even cry. There was a dull, constant ache inside me, and the silence that followed the crash seemed to echo in every corner of our home. The absence of my parents was palpable. The once familiar sounds of my mother's soft humming as she cooked or my father's steady voice offering advice were gone, replaced by a deafening quiet that filled every room.

Struggling to Cope as the Oldest Sibling

As the oldest sibling, the weight of my grief was compounded by the responsibility I felt toward my younger brothers. They were still too young to fully comprehend the magnitude of our loss. At eleven years old, I was thrust into a role I was not prepared for: the caretaker, the protector. My parents had been my foundation, and with them gone, I had to find a way to be that foundation for my brothers, even as I grappled with my own grief.

In those early days, I found myself torn between my own overwhelming sadness and the need to be strong for my brothers. I couldn't afford to break down in front of them. They needed me to be the person who held everything together. My aunt and grandmother did their best to help, but there were times when their own grief made it difficult for them to manage. My grandmother, especially, was heartbroken, having lost not only her son and daughter-in-law but also her other son, my uncle, in one tragic moment.

I found myself stepping into adult responsibilities far too early. I helped care for my brothers, doing what I could to make sure they were fed and dressed. I listened to their fears and tried to reassure them, even though I had no answers to the questions that plagued all of us. How could I explain to them why our parents were gone, why the world had taken everything from us in the blink of an eye?

Each day was a balancing act between managing my own grief and supporting my brothers. There were moments when I wanted nothing more than to disappear into my own sadness, but I couldn't allow myself that luxury. My brothers needed me, and I couldn't let them down. I was now their anchor, the one person they looked to for stability in a world that had become frightening and uncertain. And in some strange way, their dependence on me gave me a purpose, a reason to keep going, even when it felt impossible.

Moving to Sulaymaniyah with Brothers, Aunt, and Grandmother

After the accident, it became clear that we couldn't stay in Baghdad. The city was too dangerous, and the memories of my parents were too overwhelming. My aunt and grandmother decided that we would move to Sulaymaniyah, a city in the Kurdish region of Iraq, where we had relatives who could offer support. The decision to leave our home was difficult, but it was necessary for our safety and well-being.

Sulaymaniyah was a city I had only visited a few times as a child, but now it was to become our new home. We packed what little we could carry, leaving behind the house where I had grown up, where my parents had built their lives. The journey was long and arduous, filled with checkpoints and the constant fear of violence. But as we neared Sulaymaniyah, the landscape began to change. The air felt different—cooler, fresher—and the mountains that surrounded the city provided a sense of shelter, as if nature itself was offering us protection.

In Sulaymaniyah, we moved in with extended family. My aunt and grandmother tried their best to make the transition as smooth as possible for my brothers and me, but the weight of our loss followed us. Even in this new city, where the threat of war was more distant, the absence of my parents was a constant presence. My grandmother, who had always been a strong woman, seemed to age overnight. The loss of her children had drained her of her vitality, and now she moved slowly, her face etched with grief.

My aunt, too, was struggling. She had always been close to my mother, and the loss had hit her hard. Yet she did her best to take care of us, cooking meals, helping with school, and making sure we had what we needed. But I could see the sadness in her eyes, the way she would sometimes stare off into the distance, lost in her thoughts.

Sulaymaniyah was safer, but it wasn't home. It would take time for us to adjust to this new life, to the new people and routines. The city itself was more peaceful than Baghdad, and the relative calm allowed us a brief reprieve from the constant fear of violence. But grief doesn't care about geography. The pain followed us, no matter where we went.

Early Responsibilities: Caring for Siblings and Household Duties

In Sulaymaniyah, my responsibilities grew. With my aunt and grandmother dealing with their own grief, much of the daily care for my brothers fell to me. At eleven years old, I found myself taking on duties that most children my age wouldn't even think about. I helped prepare meals, cleaned the house, and made sure my brothers were taken care of. I became the one who walked them to school and helped them with their homework in the evenings. My childhood, already shattered by war and loss, had been replaced by a new role as caretaker.

These responsibilities were overwhelming at times. There were days when I felt crushed by the weight of it all, days when I wanted to run away, to escape the constant pressure. But I couldn't. My brothers depended on me, and I couldn't abandon them. I would wake up early in the morning to prepare breakfast, making sure my younger brothers were ready for school before walking them through the streets of Sulaymaniyah. I would come home to help my aunt and grandmother with household chores, trying to ease their burden even as my own grief gnawed at me.

I learned to cook simple meals, even though I had never really been taught. I had watched my mother in the kitchen before, so I tried to replicate what she used to make, hoping to bring some semblance of normalcy back into our lives. But every time I stepped into the kitchen, I was reminded of her absence, of the way she would hum softly while she worked, her hands moving expertly as she prepared meals for our family.

Taking care of my brothers also meant comforting them when they missed our parents, which was often. They would ask me questions—questions I couldn't answer—about why this had happened to us, about when things would get better. All I could do was hold them, trying to offer them the comfort and reassurance I so desperately needed myself. I tried to be strong for them, to be the rock they could rely on, but there were moments when the grief felt too heavy to bear.

Through it all, I realized that the responsibilities I had been given were shaping me. They were forcing me to grow up faster than I ever thought possible. I was no longer just a child; I was a caretaker, a provider, and a protector. And though it was a burden I had not asked for, it was one I carried because I had no other choice.

Part 2: Education and Ambitions

Chapter 4: High School and University Struggles

Completing High School in the Midst of Turmoil

The years following my family's relocation to Sulaymaniyah were a blur of emotional highs and lows. The trauma of losing my parents and uncle lingered, but life continued to march forward, indifferent to my personal grief. As I entered high school, the war in Iraq persisted, casting a long shadow over our lives. The violence that plagued the streets of Baghdad was not as pronounced in Sulaymaniyah, but the instability of the nation was a constant source of anxiety. Even in moments of calm, the uncertainty was suffocating. We never knew if or when the conflict would reach us again.

Despite the challenges, I threw myself into my studies. High school was both a refuge and a battleground. On one hand, it was a place where I could briefly escape the chaos of life at home and focus on something within my control—my education. On the other hand, it was a constant reminder of the hardships I faced outside of the classroom. My mind was frequently torn between focusing on schoolwork and worrying about my brothers, my aunt, and my grandmother. Every day was a balancing act, navigating the responsibilities of home while trying to excel academically.

I often felt like an outsider among my classmates. Many of them came from families that, while not wealthy, had a sense of stability that I had long since lost. They could afford to dream of a future without the constant reminder of survival. For me, every achievement in school felt bittersweet because I knew that the road ahead would not be easy. The pressure to succeed was immense. I wasn't just working for my future; I was working for the future of my brothers, who relied on me to be their guide and protector.

The emotional weight of my past and the ongoing financial difficulties only made high school more challenging. I often found myself studying late into the night, determined to make the most of the education I had. Failure was not an option. Education became a beacon of hope, a way out of the struggles that had defined my life since my parents' deaths. I knew that if I could do well in school, I might be able to provide a better future for my family.

Financial Hardships and Emotional Burdens

The financial situation in our household was precarious at best. My aunt did what she could to support us, but without my father's steady income, money was always tight. There were days when we weren't sure how we would manage to pay for basic necessities like food, clothing, and school supplies. The cost of living in Sulaymaniyah was lower than in Baghdad, but it was still a struggle to make ends meet. My brothers and I had learned early on to live frugally, making do with what little we had.

As the eldest, I took on small jobs wherever I could find them. Sometimes it was working in local markets, other times helping neighbors with odd tasks. Every dinar I earned went towards keeping the household afloat. It wasn't much, but it helped ease some of the burden on my aunt, who was already dealing with her own grief and responsibilities. Despite the financial struggles, she never complained. Her resilience was a source of strength for me, even when I felt like the weight of the world was on my shoulders.

But the emotional toll was even heavier than the financial strain. The grief over losing my parents never truly went away. It was always there, a constant undercurrent in my life. There were times when the sadness felt overwhelming, like a wave that threatened to pull me under. The loss of my father, mother, and uncle had left a void that could never be filled. My grandmother, who had once been a pillar of strength for our family, was now frail and broken by the loss of her children. Seeing her like that was heartbreaking. I wanted to be strong for her, but there were moments when I didn't know if I had the strength left in me.

In the midst of these hardships, I clung to my education as a lifeline. Every exam I passed, every project I completed felt like a small victory, a step closer to a future where I could take care of my family in a meaningful way. I knew that if I could succeed in school, there was a chance I could lift us out of poverty and provide my brothers with a life they deserved—a life my parents would have wanted for us.

Joining University: Pursuing a BSc in Petroleum Engineering

When I graduated from high school, it felt like a monumental achievement. It was a victory not just for me, but for my entire family. Against the odds, I had made it through. But the journey was far from over. I had always known that a university education was essential if I was going to build a better life. However, getting into university was only the first hurdle. I knew the challenges would only grow from there.

I was accepted into a program at the University of Sulaymaniyah to pursue a Bachelor of Science in Petroleum Engineering. Petroleum engineering was a field I had chosen carefully. Iraq's economy was deeply tied to its oil reserves, and I knew that a career in this industry could offer stability and financial security for my family. It wasn't just a career choice; it was a lifeline for all of us.

University life was a completely different world. The workload was intense, and I often found myself staying up late to complete assignments and prepare for exams. The subject matter was challenging—advanced mathematics, physics, geology—but I was determined to succeed. Every time I thought about giving up, I reminded myself of the sacrifices my parents had made, and of my brothers who looked up to me.

Balancing university with the ongoing responsibilities at home was difficult. There were days when it felt like I was living two lives—one as a student and the other as a caretaker. The pressure was immense, but I refused to give in. I had come too far to let my circumstances define my future. I made friends at university, but most of them didn't fully understand the weight I carried. While they worried about grades and exams, I was thinking about how to pay for my next semester or how to provide for my family.

The financial challenges didn't disappear once I entered university. Tuition was expensive, and I had to take on more part-time work to cover the costs. Scholarships were limited, and competition for them was fierce. I applied for every opportunity I could find, and while I managed to secure some financial aid, it was never enough. There were moments when I questioned whether I would be able to continue. But each time, I pushed forward, knowing that giving up wasn't an option.

Losing Grandmother During University Years

In the second year of my university studies, another tragedy struck our family. My grandmother, who had been a constant presence in our lives, passed away. Her death was a devastating blow. She had been the glue that held us together after the loss of my parents, and without her, it felt like we were once again drifting in a sea of uncertainty.

Her passing was especially hard on my aunt, who had already shouldered so much of the burden in raising us. My brothers were devastated as well. For me, it felt like losing another parent. My grandmother had been a source of comfort and wisdom, and her absence left a void that was impossible to fill. Grieving her loss while trying to keep up with my studies was one of the hardest things I had ever faced.

The emotional toll was immense, but I couldn't afford to let it derail my education. I had come too far, and my family was depending on me. My grandmother had always believed in the power of education, and I knew she would have wanted me to continue, no matter how difficult it became. So, I channeled my grief into my studies, using the memory of her strength to push me forward.

As I navigated the rest of my university years, I carried the weight of loss with me. But I also carried the hope that one day, I could build a better future for my brothers and honor the sacrifices of those we had lost. The journey was far from over, but I knew that with each passing day, I was getting closer to realizing that dream.

Chapter 5: A Bachelor's Degree Without a Future

Graduation and the Struggle to Find a Job

The day I graduated from the University of Sulaymaniyah with a Bachelor's degree in Petroleum Engineering should have been one of the happiest moments of my life. After years of sacrifice, hard work, and persistence, I had achieved something that many in my situation would have given up on. I had pushed through the grief of losing my parents and grandmother, navigated financial struggles, and balanced my responsibilities at home with the demands of university. I had succeeded against the odds, and I should have been proud.

Yet, when I walked across that stage and held my degree in my hands, there was a gnawing feeling of uncertainty. Iraq's economy was in disarray, and the petroleum industry, once the backbone of the nation, was suffering under the weight of political instability and global market fluctuations. The war had decimated much of the country's infrastructure, and the job market was bleak for recent graduates, even in fields as critical as petroleum engineering.

As I celebrated with my classmates, I couldn't help but feel an undercurrent of anxiety. We were all stepping into a world that was drastically different from the one we had envisioned when we started our degrees. The job market was flooded with graduates, and the opportunities were few and far between. I knew that finding a job in my field would be difficult, but I didn't realize just how challenging it would become.

The Relentless Job Search: 1000 Emails, No Replies

After graduation, the reality of the situation hit me like a ton of bricks. With my degree in hand, I began the grueling process of searching for employment. At first, I was hopeful. I had a solid academic background and relevant skills. I had even completed internships during my university years, gaining practical experience in the field. Surely, I thought, that would set me apart.

I began sending out job applications, carefully crafting each cover letter and tailoring my resume to fit the specific requirements of every position I applied for. At first, I focused on local opportunities, thinking that starting in Iraq would give me a chance to build experience before looking abroad. But the oil and gas industry in Iraq was in decline. Political unrest, corruption, and the ongoing impact of war had crippled much of the sector, leaving only a handful of opportunities for recent graduates.

Weeks turned into months, and the emails I sent seemed to vanish into a void. I checked my inbox obsessively, hoping for even a single reply—some indication that my applications were being considered. But there was nothing. No replies, no callbacks, no interviews. The silence was deafening.

Desperate to find any opportunity, I expanded my search beyond Iraq. I started applying to companies across the Middle East, Europe, and even the United States. I sent out emails to every major oil company and engineering firm I could think of. I applied to small startups, government positions, and research institutions. By the end of the first year, I had sent out over 1000 applications.

The rejection was relentless. Most of the time, I didn't even receive a response. On the rare occasion when I did, it was always the same: "Thank you for your interest, but we regret to inform you that we have selected another candidate." Every rejection felt like a personal failure, a confirmation that I wasn't good enough. I began to doubt everything—my degree, my abilities, my future.

Financially, things were growing dire. My part-time jobs barely covered basic expenses, and my family was still dependent on me. I had hoped that by this point, I would have found a stable job that would allow me to support my brothers and provide them with the opportunities they deserved. Instead, I found myself in limbo, unable to move forward and haunted by the fear that all of my efforts had been for nothing.

Decision to Pursue a Master's Degree Abroad

As the months dragged on and the job rejections continued to pile up, I realized I had to make a difficult decision. The oil industry was not recovering anytime soon, and staying in Iraq meant continuing to fight an uphill battle. I knew that if I wanted to improve my chances of securing a meaningful career, I needed to expand my skill set and gain international experience.

The idea of pursuing a master's degree began to take root. A master's degree would allow me to specialize in a niche area of petroleum engineering or expand into a related field like renewable energy, which was becoming increasingly important on the global stage. It would also give me the chance to study and network abroad, increasing my chances of finding employment outside Iraq's struggling economy.

But the decision wasn't an easy one. Pursuing a master's degree meant another two years of financial strain, with no guarantee that it would lead to a job. I would need to find a way to fund my studies, apply to universities, and leave my family behind at a time when they still depended on me. The thought of leaving my brothers and aunt behind weighed heavily on my heart. I had been their anchor for so long, and the idea of being separated from them was painful.

But I also knew that staying in Iraq wasn't a viable option. I had to think about the long-term future, not just for myself, but for my family as well. If I could succeed abroad and find stable employment, I could eventually provide them with a better life. It was a risk, but it was one I felt I had to take.

I began researching master's programs around the world. I focused on countries with strong oil industries, such as Norway, Canada, and the United Kingdom. Each application required careful preparation—letters of recommendation, personal statements, and proof of financial capability. It was a daunting process, but it gave me a renewed sense of purpose.

Eventually, I received an offer from a prestigious university in Europe. It was an opportunity to study under some of the leading experts in the field and gain the international exposure I needed. The tuition was expensive, but I managed to secure a partial scholarship that would cover a portion of the costs. For the rest, I would have to rely on loans and part-time work.

With a mixture of hope and fear, I accepted the offer. It was a leap of faith, but one that I believed would lead to a brighter future. I knew the road ahead would be difficult, but after everything I had been through, I was no stranger to challenges. I was ready to take the next step in my journey, even if it meant leaving behind everything I had ever known.

As I packed my bags and prepared to leave Iraq, I couldn't help but feel a pang of sadness. I was leaving behind my family, my home, and the life I had built. But I was also stepping into a new chapter, one filled with the promise of opportunity. It wasn't just about finding a job anymore—it was about reclaiming my future.

Chapter 6: Abroad for the Master's Degree

Going Abroad for an MSc in Petroleum and Natural Gas Engineering

In 2018, I left Iraq to pursue an MSc in Petroleum and Natural Gas Engineering at a prestigious university in Europe. It was a monumental decision—one that filled me with both excitement and trepidation. I had worked tirelessly to secure a place in the program, and now I was stepping into a world of new opportunities, challenges, and uncertainty. Leaving behind my family, especially my brothers, was the hardest part. But I carried with me the hope that this path would finally open doors for me and ultimately secure a better future for all of us.

Arriving in a foreign country was an overwhelming experience. I found myself surrounded by different cultures, languages, and customs. The university itself was a world-class institution, with state-of-the-art laboratories and a diverse cohort of students from across the globe. It was exhilarating to be in an environment where cutting-edge research was being conducted, and where I would have the chance to learn from some of the leading experts in petroleum engineering.

However, the excitement of being in a new place was quickly tempered by the reality of my situation. The cost of living in Europe was far higher than I had anticipated, and despite the partial scholarship I had received, I found myself struggling to make ends meet. Rent, food, textbooks, transportation—everything added up quickly, and my limited savings began to dwindle. I took on part-time jobs where I could, working late into the night at cafes or restaurants just to scrape together enough to cover my basic expenses.

Financial Struggles, Family Support, and Reckless Spending Habits

Despite my financial challenges, I was determined to support my family back home. My brothers were still young and needed my help. My aunt, who had cared for us after the loss of our parents, was doing her best, but the weight of providing for the household fell on me. Every month, I would send as much money as I could back to Iraq, often leaving myself with barely enough to get by.

But I wasn't always wise with my spending. The stress of managing my finances and the pressure of my academic workload sometimes led me to make impulsive decisions. There were nights when, after a grueling day of classes and work, I would treat myself to meals at expensive restaurants or splurge on things I didn't really need. It was my way of coping with the constant stress and homesickness. But those moments of indulgence only added to my financial burdens, forcing me to work even harder just to stay afloat.

The financial strain began to take a toll on my mental health. There were days when I felt completely overwhelmed, unsure if I could continue balancing the demands of my studies with the pressure of supporting my family. I was constantly worried about money, about my academic performance, and about whether or not I had made the right decision in leaving Iraq. But every time I spoke to my brothers, they reminded me of why I was doing this. They believed in me, and I couldn't let them down.

Completing the Master's During the COVID-19 Pandemic

Just as I was beginning to find my footing, the world was hit by the COVID-19 pandemic in early 2020. Almost overnight, life as I knew it changed. The university shut down, classes were moved online, and the part-time jobs I relied on disappeared as businesses closed their doors. The isolation was intense—far from home, in a foreign country, and now unable to even interact with my classmates or professors in person. I was confined to my small apartment, where the walls seemed to close in on me as the days stretched into weeks and then months.

The pandemic made an already difficult situation even harder. With the global economy in free fall, the job prospects in the petroleum industry looked bleaker than ever. The uncertainty about what the future held was suffocating. Many of my fellow students were in the same boat, struggling with the weight of financial worries, the fear of illness, and the stress of completing their degrees under unprecedented circumstances.

Despite the challenges, I pressed on. My professors were understanding, offering support where they could, and the university provided resources for students affected by the pandemic. But it was up to me to find the strength to keep going. I buried myself in my studies, focusing on completing my coursework and starting my thesis. The thesis, which was the culmination of my master's program, became both my escape and my burden. It was my opportunity to showcase everything I had learned, but it was also a monumental task to undertake in the middle of a global crisis.

I spent countless hours researching, writing, and revising. The subject of my thesis focused on the impact of emerging technologies on the efficiency of petroleum extraction in a post-COVID world—an ironically timely topic. As the pandemic dragged on, I poured my energy into the project, determined to finish what I had started.

Online Thesis Defense and Return Home (2020)

By the time summer rolled around, it was time to defend my thesis. Normally, this would have been a formal, in-person presentation in front of a panel of professors, but due to the pandemic, everything was conducted online. I sat in my apartment, dressed in my best suit, nervously awaiting the start of my virtual defense. My laptop was my only connection to the outside world, and through it, I would present the work I had spent months preparing.

The defense was nerve-wracking, to say the least. The professors asked tough questions, pushing me to explain my research in detail and justify my conclusions. But despite the technical glitches and the anxiety of speaking to a screen, I managed to get through it. When it was over, I sat in stunned silence, hardly able to believe that I had completed my master's degree in the midst of such chaos.

With my degree in hand, I made the decision to return home to Iraq in late 2020. The pandemic had disrupted job markets worldwide, and staying in Europe without employment prospects didn't seem feasible. My family needed me, and I longed to be with them after so many years apart. The return home was bittersweet—on one hand, I was relieved to be back with my loved ones, but on the other, I felt the weight of uncertainty once again.

What would the future hold for someone with a degree in petroleum engineering during a global crisis? Could I find a job in an industry that seemed to be teetering on the edge of collapse? Despite these lingering questions, one thing was clear: I had come too far to give up now. The path ahead might be uncertain, but I was determined to keep moving forward, no matter how difficult the journey.

Part 3: The Job and the Dream

Chapter 7: A Lifeline—Becoming a Tax Accountant

Unable to Find Work in Petroleum, Pivoting to Tax Accounting

After returning to Iraq in late 2020, I found myself at a crossroads. The world was still reeling from the COVID-19 pandemic, and the petroleum industry, which had once been booming, was now facing unprecedented challenges. Despite having earned a master's degree in Petroleum and Natural Gas Engineering, I quickly realized that job opportunities in my field were few and far between. Every day, I scoured job boards, sent out countless applications, and waited for responses that never came. It was a demoralizing experience. All the hard work, sacrifices, and struggles I had endured seemed to be in vain. The dream of working in my chosen field felt increasingly distant.

But life has a way of presenting unexpected opportunities. While searching for jobs in engineering, I began to consider alternative career paths. One day, I came across a listing for a tax accounting position at a UK-based company. At first glance, it seemed like an odd fit for someone with my background. I had no formal training in finance or accounting, and the idea of pivoting to an entirely new field felt daunting. But the more I thought about it, the more it made sense. I needed a job—any job—that would allow me to support my family and make use of my analytical skills. After years of searching, I realized that I couldn't afford to be picky.

With no prior experience in tax accounting, I threw myself into learning everything I could about the field. I spent hours each day reading textbooks, taking online courses, and watching tutorials on tax laws and financial management. It was an entirely new world, but one that appealed to the logical, problem-solving side of me. I found that many of the skills I had developed as an engineer—attention to detail, critical thinking, and data analysis—were transferable to accounting. Slowly but surely, I began to build a foundation of knowledge.

Learning Finance and Passing the Interview for a UK-Based Company

After weeks of studying, I felt ready to apply for the tax accounting position. The interview process was nerve-wracking. I knew I lacked formal experience in the field, but I was determined to demonstrate my willingness to learn and adapt. During the interview, I was honest about my background, explaining how the economic downturn had forced me to consider new career paths. I emphasized my strong work ethic, my ability to learn quickly, and my deep understanding of complex systems—qualities that I believed would serve me well in the world of finance.

To my surprise and relief, the interviewers were impressed. They appreciated my honesty and resilience in pivoting from engineering to finance, especially under difficult circumstances. They were looking for someone with a strong analytical mind, someone who could learn on the job and adapt to new challenges. A few days later, I received the news that I had been offered the position. I had secured my first full-time job in years, and though it wasn't in the field I had originally envisioned, it was a lifeline.

Gratitude for the Life-Changing Remote Job Opportunity

The job was remote, which was a blessing in more ways than one. Working from home meant that I could stay in Iraq with my family while earning a stable income from an international company. In a time of global uncertainty, the remote nature of the job provided a sense of security. I no longer had to worry about the volatility of the petroleum industry or the challenges of finding work in a competitive market. Instead, I had found a new path—one that allowed me to provide for my loved ones and build a future.

I was deeply grateful for the opportunity. Not only did the job offer financial stability, but it also gave me a sense of purpose. For the first time in years, I felt like I was moving forward again. I threw myself into my work, learning the intricacies of tax accounting, international finance, and compliance regulations. Every day brought new challenges, but I was eager to prove myself and grow in this unfamiliar field.

Four Years of Work, Growing Professionally and Financially

As the years passed, I grew more confident in my abilities as a tax accountant. The company I worked for was supportive, offering training programs and opportunities for professional development. I took full advantage of these resources, enrolling in courses and earning certifications that allowed me to deepen my knowledge and expand my skill set. Over time, I became an integral part of the team, taking on more responsibilities and handling increasingly complex accounts.

The financial benefits were significant. After years of struggling to make ends meet, I was finally able to provide a comfortable life for my family. I helped pay for my brothers' education, supported my aunt, and began saving for the future. The stability that this job provided allowed me to breathe easier, knowing that I no longer had to worry about how I would make it through the month.

Professionally, the experience was transformative. While I had initially seen the job as a temporary solution, I soon realized that I was developing a genuine interest in finance. I enjoyed the intellectual challenges that came with tax accounting, from navigating complex regulations to finding creative solutions for clients. The analytical mindset I had honed as an engineer served me well in this new field, and I discovered a passion for helping others manage their finances.

As I reflect on those four years of work, I see them as a period of growth and resilience. What had started as a desperate pivot became an unexpected success. I learned that life doesn't always go according to plan, but sometimes, the detours lead to opportunities you never imagined. My journey into tax accounting was not part of my original dream, but it became a lifeline that helped me rebuild my life and support the people I love. And for that, I will always be grateful.

Chapter 8: The European Misadventure

The Dream of Immigrating to Europe for a Better Life

The desire to immigrate to Europe had always lingered in the back of my mind. As a young boy, I had been captivated by stories of distant lands filled with opportunities and prosperity. My experience as a tax accountant had provided me with a level of financial stability, I had never thought possible. However, the longing for a more adventurous life, free from the uncertainties and challenges of Iraq, started to burn brighter than ever. I envisioned a fresh start in a country where I could thrive both personally and professionally.

After much deliberation and encouragement from family and friends, I decided to pursue this dream. I began to research potential countries in Europe that welcomed immigrants. The idea of experiencing new cultures, expanding my horizons, and ultimately building a better future for my family and me was incredibly appealing. I set my sights on countries that had strong economies and opportunities for skilled workers like myself, focusing on places where I could leverage my background in engineering and accounting.

Initial Struggles: Currency Exchange Mishap, Nights Spent Outdoors

Excitement coursed through me as I made preparations for my journey. I meticulously saved every penny, knowing that financial stability would be crucial for my initial months abroad. However, my first misstep came before I even boarded my flight. I had exchanged a significant number of Iraqi dinars for euros, convinced that I had secured a favorable rate. Unfortunately, the currency exchange shop I chose was not reputable, and I ended up losing a substantial portion of my savings in the transaction.

Arriving in Europe with less money than anticipated, the reality of my situation began to sink in. My plan had been to find temporary accommodation while I secured a job, but the dwindling funds made it increasingly difficult to find a place to stay. I often found myself wandering the streets, searching for hostels or inexpensive lodging, only to be turned away due to lack of funds. Some nights, I had no choice but to sleep outdoors, finding shelter in public parks or along busy streets, clinging to the hope that tomorrow would bring better fortune.

Getting Scammed with Fake Documents for Canada

In my desperation, I became susceptible to the promises of unscrupulous individuals who preyed on immigrants like me. One day, while seeking guidance from a group of expatriates, I was introduced to someone claiming to have connections to immigration services in Canada. They convinced me that I could secure a fast-track visa if I paid a substantial fee for their "services." Desperate and blinded by hope, I transferred a significant amount of money, believing I was taking a step closer to my dream.

Days turned into weeks, and I realized I had been scammed. The documents I received were nothing more than poorly crafted fakes, and the promised visa was a mirage. I was crushed—not just financially but emotionally. The stress of my circumstances had already taken a toll, and now I faced the bitter reality of being cheated. I felt foolish and ashamed, questioning my judgment and ability to navigate this new world. The dream of a better life seemed further away than ever, and I was paralyzed by despair.

Financial Ruin and Emotional Exhaustion

The financial burden of the scam deepened my predicament. With dwindling funds and no prospects for employment, I quickly fell into a state of financial ruin. Every day became a struggle for basic necessities. I rationed food, often going hungry to save money, and relied on public facilities for basic hygiene. My emotional exhaustion compounded the situation; the initial thrill of my adventure was replaced with a gnawing anxiety about my future.

The pressure to find a solution weighed heavily on my shoulders. I felt like I was drowning in a sea of despair, unable to see a way out. Every rejection I faced felt like a reminder of my failures. The dream that had once inspired me now felt like a cruel joke. I grappled with feelings of isolation, far from the support network I had in Iraq. I was thousands of miles away from family and friends, with only my own resolve to keep me afloat.

Relying on Family and Friends for Rescue

As my situation grew more dire, I reluctantly reached out to family and friends back home. I shared my struggles and the reality of my circumstances, explaining how I had lost money and hope in this quest for a better life. It was difficult to admit my failures, but I knew I needed their support more than ever. To my relief, my family responded with compassion and understanding. They rallied together, pooling resources to send me financial assistance.

With their help, I was able to afford temporary accommodations and some basic necessities. I felt an overwhelming sense of gratitude toward those who had supported me during my darkest hours. Their unwavering faith in me reignited the flicker of hope I had nearly extinguished. My family's belief in my potential reminded me that I was not alone in this journey.

Slowly, with their support and encouragement, I began to rebuild my life. I resumed my job search, reaching out to every possible connection I had made during my time in Europe. I leaned on the lessons learned from my past experiences, determined to emerge stronger from this ordeal. Each day was a new challenge, but with my family by my side, I regained a sense of purpose and direction.

The European misadventure was a stark reminder of the unpredictability of life. It taught me that dreams can be fragile and that the path to success is often riddled with obstacles. While the initial experience was filled with hardship and loss, it ultimately became a transformative chapter in my life. I learned the importance of resilience, the strength of family bonds, and the necessity of relying on the support of others during difficult times.

Though my vision of Europe had changed, the journey had not been in vain. I emerged from this misadventure with a renewed sense of determination and a deeper understanding of the value of community and family. While the dream of a better life remained, I realized that the journey itself was just as important as the destination. And with this newfound clarity, I was ready to embrace whatever came next, knowing that I could weather any storm as long as I had the support of those who loved me.

Chapter 9: An Angel Named Nicole

Meeting Nicole, an Online Friend of Six Years

In the midst of my struggles, a glimmer of light broke through the clouds when I received a message from Nicole, a friend I had met online six years prior. We had connected through a mutual interest in engineering and technology, bonding over late-night conversations about our dreams, aspirations, and the challenges we faced in our respective lives. Though we had never met in person, our friendship had blossomed through countless chats, shared experiences, and mutual encouragement.

Nicole had been a steady presence in my life, offering support during my darkest days. As my situation in Europe deteriorated, she remained unwavering in her belief that I would eventually find my way. Now, hearing her voice in a video call filled me with warmth and excitement. She mentioned that she would be visiting Europe soon and suggested that we finally meet. The idea of seeing her face-to-face felt surreal. I had long imagined this moment, and now it was finally happening.

Four Unforgettable Days in Europe: Beaches, Museums, Cinema, and Friendship

When the day of our meeting arrived, I was a bundle of nerves and excitement. We arranged to meet at a beautiful beachside café, and as I approached, I spotted her sitting at a table, her smile radiant against the backdrop of azure waves. The moment we saw each other, all the distance and digital barriers melted away. It felt as though we were old friends reuniting after years apart.

Our four days together were nothing short of magical. We spent countless hours exploring the vibrant streets of the city, laughing and sharing stories as we wandered through bustling markets and quaint neighborhoods. Nicole introduced me to local delicacies, and we savored every bite, our taste buds dancing with delight. We strolled along the picturesque coastline, where the sun dipped below the horizon, painting the sky in hues of orange and pink. Those sunsets became a canvas for our conversations, each moment imbued with a sense of wonder and possibility.

We visited renowned museums, immersing ourselves in art and history. Nicole's enthusiasm for creativity inspired me, and I found myself captivated by the masterpieces that surrounded us. We debated the meanings behind various artworks, each discussion revealing more about our personalities and dreams. It was a chance to connect on a deeper level, exploring not just the world around us but the landscapes of our minds.

One of the highlights of our trip was a spontaneous cinema night. We decided to watch an indie film at a local theater, a hidden gem that Nicole had discovered online. The film was thought-provoking and resonated with both of us, touching on themes of resilience and the pursuit of dreams. We laughed, cried, and held discussions late into the night, sharing our own aspirations and fears, creating memories that felt timeless.

Renewed Hope and Bittersweet Goodbyes

As our time together drew to a close, I couldn't help but feel a bittersweet twinge in my heart. The four days had flown by, and the friendship that had blossomed through screens now felt as tangible as the ocean breeze. Nicole had become my confidante, my cheerleader, and my anchor during the storm of uncertainty. Her presence ignited a renewed sense of hope within me—a belief that my dreams were still attainable, despite the setbacks I had faced.

On our final evening, we sat on the beach, the sound of waves crashing against the shore serving as a soothing backdrop. The sun had set, leaving behind a canopy of stars. We spoke about our futures, sharing our aspirations and the paths we envisioned taking. In those moments, I felt as though the weight of my past struggles had lifted, replaced by a sense of clarity and direction.

When it was time to say goodbye, tears welled in my eyes. I hugged Nicole tightly, cherishing the warmth of our friendship. We promised to stay in touch, vowing to support each other from afar. As she walked away,

I felt a sense of gratitude wash over me. Nicole had come into my life like an angel, reminding me of the beauty of connection and the importance of friendship.

Her visit had transformed my perspective, reigniting my passion for life and my dreams. I returned to my reality, carrying the memories of our adventures and the renewed hope she had gifted me. Though the road ahead remained uncertain, I now understood that I was not alone. With the support of my family and friends, including Nicole, I was ready to face whatever challenges lay ahead.

This chapter in my life became a testament to the power of friendship and the profound impact one person can have on another. Nicole was not just a friend; she was a beacon of light in my journey, and I vowed to carry her spirit with me as I continued to navigate the complexities of life in a new world.

Chapter 10: The Journey Home

Voluntary Return Home After a Challenging Time Abroad

After four unforgettable days with Nicole, I made the difficult decision to return home to Iraq. My time in Europe had been a whirlwind of emotions, but the struggles I faced—financial ruin, emotional exhaustion, and a sense of dislocation—had taken their toll. I had arrived in Europe with dreams of a better life, only to confront a harsh reality that tested my resilience and determination.

As I packed my belongings, I felt a mixture of sadness and relief. While I was leaving behind the memories of my brief adventure and the hope it had reignited, I was also aware that I was heading back to a place filled with familiarity, love, and support. I had realized that the dream of a better life did not solely depend on geographical boundaries; it could also be found in the embrace of family and friends who had always believed in me.

The flight home felt surreal. I sat by the window, watching the clouds drift beneath me, reflecting on the journey I had taken thus far. Each passing moment brought a sense of closure to my European misadventure, a chapter that had been fraught with challenges yet rich with lessons. I reminded myself that returning home was not a sign of defeat; rather, it was an opportunity to regroup, reflect, and rebuild.

The Feeling of Relief and Comfort Upon Returning to Family and Friends

As the plane touched down at Erbil International Airport, I was overwhelmed with a wave of emotions. The familiar sights, sounds, and scents of home enveloped me like a warm blanket. Stepping off the plane, I felt a sense of relief wash over me, a feeling of comfort I had longed for during my turbulent time abroad. My heart raced with anticipation as I made my way through the terminal, eager to reunite with my family and friends.

When I finally saw my brothers waiting for me at the arrivals gate, I rushed into their arms, laughter and tears mingling in the air. They had been my anchors during the storms of grief and loss, and their unwavering support had kept me grounded. My aunt and grandmother, who had played pivotal roles in my upbringing, joined us, their faces lit up with joy.

We shared stories of our respective journeys, the laughter punctuated by moments of solemn reflection. My family welcomed me back with open arms, and I felt the heaviness of the past months lift, replaced by a renewed sense of belonging.

Rejoining the UK-Based Company, Rebuilding Life from Scratch

As I settled back into life in Sulaymaniyah, I was determined to rebuild from scratch. I had been fortunate to maintain my position with the UK-based tax accounting firm during my time abroad. They had offered me a remote position that allowed me to continue my work while also providing the flexibility I needed to navigate my personal challenges.

Returning to work felt both exhilarating and daunting. I had to adapt to a new routine while managing the emotional residue of my experiences abroad. But the support of my colleagues, many of whom I had connected with over the years, made the transition smoother. I was grateful for the opportunity to contribute to projects that mattered, and I threw myself into my work with renewed vigor.

In my spare time, I began to reconnect with my community. I volunteered at local organizations that supported those in need, driven by a desire to give back and help others who might be struggling. Through these experiences, I learned the importance of resilience and the power of community. The friendships I had formed back home reminded me that I was not alone in this journey.

The journey home was not just a return to a physical location; it was a rediscovery of who I was and what I stood for. I began to reassess my dreams, realizing that my past struggles had shaped my ambitions in profound ways. I set new goals for myself—both personally and professionally—seeking a path that would allow me to flourish.

Through the challenges I faced, I emerged with a stronger sense of identity and purpose. My experiences abroad had taught me valuable lessons about adaptability, perseverance, and the importance of community. As I looked toward the future, I felt a renewed sense of hope, ready to face whatever lay ahead, knowing that I had the love and support of my family and friends to guide me along the way.

The journey home marked the beginning of a new chapter, one filled with possibilities, dreams, and a deeper understanding of what it means to belong. It was time to write the next part of my story—a story of resilience, ambition, and the unwavering belief that no matter where life takes you, home is where the heart is.

Chapter 11: Becoming a Lecturer

New Beginnings: Teaching Part-Time at a University in Kurdistan

As I continued to rebuild my life in Sulaymaniyah, an unexpected opportunity arose: a part-time teaching position at a local university in Kurdistan. Initially, the idea of becoming a lecturer had never crossed my mind. My focus had primarily been on my career in tax accounting, but the chance to share my knowledge with the next generation of students intrigued me. I believed that my own educational journey, marked by challenges and triumphs, could resonate with young minds eager to learn.

I applied for the position, unsure of what to expect. When I received the offer, a mixture of excitement and apprehension filled me. I had always admired teachers who inspired students, igniting their curiosity and passion for learning. Now, I would have the chance to be that catalyst for others.

The first day of class was a whirlwind of emotions. As I stood before a room full of eager faces, I felt a rush of adrenaline mixed with nostalgia. I was reminded of my own experiences as a student—those moments of enlightenment when a concept clicked or a lesson inspired a new way of thinking. I knew I wanted to create an environment that fostered curiosity and encouraged students to challenge themselves.

The Joy of Connecting with Students and Sharing Knowledge

As the weeks turned into months, I found immense joy in my role as a lecturer. Each class became a platform for dialogue and exploration, where students felt comfortable asking questions and engaging in discussions. I strived to create an atmosphere of collaboration, where we could learn from one another.

Teaching became a profound source of fulfillment. I watched my students grow, not only academically but also as individuals. Their enthusiasm for learning reignited my own passion for education. I often shared stories from my life, illustrating how perseverance and resilience could lead to success despite adversity. I emphasized the importance of critical thinking and problem-solving, skills that I believed were essential in today's rapidly changing world.

I developed strong connections with many of my students. Their diverse backgrounds and unique perspectives enriched the classroom experience. I encouraged them to share their own stories, fostering an environment of empathy and understanding. These interactions reminded me of the power of education; it wasn't just about imparting knowledge but about inspiring the next generation to dream big and pursue their passions.

Reflections on the Journey: From Tragedy to Teaching

Reflecting on my journey thus far, I recognized the profound transformation I had undergone. From the heart-wrenching loss of my parents and uncle to the struggles of rebuilding my life after a turbulent time abroad, each experience had shaped me into the person I had become. Teaching allowed me to channel my grief and experiences into something meaningful.

In the quiet moments after class, I often took time to reflect on my path. I thought about the childhood dreams that had once seemed so distant and how the trials I had faced had only fueled my determination to succeed. I realized that my journey was not merely a story of survival; it was also a testament to the human spirit's resilience.

As I walked through the university halls, I felt a sense of belonging that had eluded me for so long. I was no longer just a survivor of tragedy; I was a mentor, a guide, and a source of inspiration for my students. I often reminded them that education is not just about acquiring knowledge; it's about discovering oneself, understanding the world, and finding one's place in it.

The classroom became a sanctuary—a space where I could contribute positively to the lives of others. I witnessed the light in my students' eyes when they grasped a challenging concept or shared their own experiences. These moments reaffirmed my belief that education holds the power to transform lives and uplift communities.

As I continued on this new path, I remained grateful for the opportunities that life had presented me. Teaching was not just a job; it was a calling—a chance to give back to a community that had supported me during my most challenging times. I understood that my journey from tragedy to teaching was not just a personal triumph; it was a story that I could share with my students, encouraging them to find strength in their own narratives and to embrace the challenges that lay ahead.

In this chapter of my life, I embraced the role of a teacher with open arms, knowing that the lessons I imparted would go far beyond textbooks. Together with my students, I was embarking on a journey of discovery, growth, and endless possibilities—a journey filled with hope, resilience, and the unwavering belief in the power of education.

Chapter 12: Brothers, Bonds, and Dreams

Supporting Brothers Through Their Struggles and Aspirations

In the wake of our family's tragedies, my brothers and I formed a bond that transcended the typical fraternal relationship. Each of us carried our scars, shaped by the loss of our parents and the weight of our new realities. My role as the eldest sibling naturally positioned me as a pillar of support for my younger brothers, Mahmood and Samir, who each faced their own battles in the aftermath of our family's upheaval.

Mahmood, the middle brother, was grappling with the pressures of adolescence while mourning the loss of our parents. He had always been a bright student, but the shadows of grief loomed over him, impacting his performance in school. I took it upon myself to spend more time with him, helping with homework and encouraging him to pursue his interests. I saw in him a passion for art, a skill he had not yet fully explored. I enrolled him in a local art workshop, hoping it would serve as an outlet for his emotions and a space where he could reconnect with joy.

Samir, the youngest, was only a child when tragedy struck. He often felt lost, unable to fully comprehend the magnitude of what we had lost. I made it a priority to engage him in activities that brought him happiness. We spent countless afternoons playing soccer in the neighborhood park, laughing and joking as if nothing had happened. I wanted him to know that despite our family's past, there was still room for laughter and dreams.

As I watched my brothers navigate their struggles, I felt a profound sense of responsibility. I wanted to be there for them, to guide them through the uncertainties of life, and to help them chase their aspirations. My own journey had taught me that while adversity could dim our spirits, it could also ignite a fierce determination to rise above.

Sacrificing for Family: Balancing Dreams and Responsibilities

As much as I wanted to support my brothers in their pursuits, the reality of our situation demanded sacrifices. The financial burdens weighed heavily on my shoulders, and my work as a tax accountant became the primary source of income for our household. I often found myself juggling my job with the responsibilities of caring for my brothers, ensuring they had everything they needed while still striving to achieve my own dreams.

Balancing work and family was no easy feat. There were nights when I would stay up late, grading papers for my students or preparing lesson plans, only to wake up early to take Mahmood to school. I would often skip meals, sacrificing my own well-being for the sake of my brothers. Yet, deep down, I knew that these sacrifices were necessary. I drew strength from the love I had for my family and the desire to see my brothers thrive.

In those moments of struggle, I often reflected on my father's words: "Family is everything, and the strength of our bond will carry us through the toughest times." His wisdom resonated with me, reminding me that our connection as brothers was not just a source of support but also a powerful motivator to keep moving forward.

Navigating Life's Uncertainties with the Memory of a Father's Words

Life, with its unpredictability, often threw challenges our way. There were times when I doubted my ability to provide for my brothers, and moments when I felt overwhelmed by the weight of responsibility. But my father's memory was a guiding light. I kept a small photograph of him on my desk—a reminder of the man who had instilled in me the values of hard work, perseverance, and family unity.

Whenever I faced moments of uncertainty, I would look at that photograph and feel a surge of determination. My father's words echoed in my mind, encouraging me to embrace challenges head-on. I realized that my journey was not just about me anymore; it was about us as a family. I wanted to honor my parents' legacy by ensuring that my brothers had the opportunities they deserved, even if it meant putting my own dreams on hold.

As Mahmood blossomed in his art classes, I took pride in supporting his aspirations. I arranged for him to showcase his work at local exhibitions, where he garnered praise and encouragement from our community. Seeing him succeed fueled my desire to help Samir discover his own passions. I enrolled him in extracurricular activities, exposing him to various fields to find what ignited his enthusiasm.

The bond we shared was more than just brotherhood; it was a commitment to lifting each other up and nurturing one another's dreams. We often held late-night conversations, discussing our hopes for the future and the paths we envisioned for ourselves. These moments became sacred, a testament to our resilience and unwavering support for one another.

The Power of Brotherhood

Through the struggles, we learned to rely on each other. The nights spent laughing and dreaming together became our refuge from the harsh realities of life. We created a family culture of resilience, where every setback was met with renewed determination. I emphasized the importance of education, encouraging my brothers to pursue their studies diligently, as I knew that knowledge would empower them to shape their futures.

With time, we began to carve out our own identities. Mahmood's art flourished, and he started to gain recognition for his work. Samir, inspired by his older brothers, began to show interest in technology, spending hours tinkering with gadgets and learning programming skills. It filled me with joy to see their passions develop, knowing that I had played a part in nurturing their aspirations.

Looking back on our journey, I recognized the profound bond that had formed between us. The struggles we had faced only strengthened our connection. We were no longer just brothers; we were a team, navigating the complexities of life together. Each triumph, no matter how small, became a shared victory, reminding us of the resilience we inherited from our parents.

As we moved forward, I remained committed to my brothers and our shared dreams. The path ahead was still uncertain, but with each other's support and the memory of our father guiding us, I knew we would continue to rise. The bonds we had forged were unbreakable, and together, we would strive to fulfill our dreams while honoring the legacy of our family.

Part 5: Reflections and Lessons

Chapter 13: The Cost of Survival

The Economic Struggles of Life in Kurdistan

Living in Kurdistan, the weight of economic struggles is a constant companion. The echoes of war have left deep scars on the region, creating an environment where survival is often a daily battle. As I navigated adulthood and assumed responsibility for my brothers, I became acutely aware of the harsh realities we faced. Jobs were scarce, and those that existed rarely offered fair wages, forcing many families, including ours, into a state of financial insecurity.

Each month brought its own set of challenges. Rent was a significant burden, and the price of basic necessities fluctuated unpredictably. We often had to make difficult choices: should we prioritize groceries or the electricity bill? These decisions were painful, but they also fostered a resilience that became a part of our identity. I learned to stretch every dinar, to find creative ways to make do with what we had. From repurposing old furniture to growing vegetables in our small garden, I discovered that even the simplest acts could offer a sense of control in an otherwise chaotic environment.

In Kurdistan, the economic struggles were not just personal; they were a reflection of the larger societal issues stemming from decades of conflict. Many families were left shattered, their hopes for a better life overshadowed by the ruins of war. I witnessed friends and neighbors facing similar hardships, their dreams deferred as they battled the same systemic challenges. This shared experience fostered a sense of solidarity among us, reminding me that we were not alone in our struggles.

The Wider Global Context of War, Survival, and Hope

The struggles I faced were not unique to Kurdistan. They resonated within a broader global context, where countless individuals and families grappled with the effects of war and economic instability. As I reflected on our situation, I found myself drawn to stories from around the world—stories of resilience in the face of adversity, of communities coming together to support one another.

In many ways, the fight for survival transcended borders. Refugees from war-torn countries sought refuge in foreign lands, often encountering hostility and discrimination. Their stories echoed our own struggles, highlighting the universal longing for safety, dignity, and a better life. I learned that, despite our differences, our shared humanity united us in our quest for hope and resilience.

I began to engage more deeply with these global narratives, finding solace in the knowledge that we were part of a larger tapestry of survival. I participated in community events and forums that raised awareness about the challenges faced by displaced populations, discovering the power of collective action in the fight for justice and equality. Each story I encountered served as a reminder that while our paths may differ, the fundamental desire for a brighter future is a common thread that binds us all.

Finding Beauty in the Smallest Moments

Amidst the chaos and uncertainty, I learned to find beauty in the smallest moments. The simple pleasures of life became my refuge, grounding me when the weight of survival felt overwhelming. A steaming cup of tea on a cold morning, the warmth of the sun on my face, or the sound of laughter echoing through our home brought me joy and reminded me of the preciousness of life.

One evening, as I sat on our balcony watching the sunset paint the sky in hues of orange and pink, I felt a deep sense of gratitude wash over me. In that moment, I realized that even amidst struggle, there were moments of tranquility and beauty. I called my brothers to join me, and we sat in silence, absorbing the beauty of the world around us. It was a small moment, but it anchored us, reminding us that life continued to offer gifts despite the hardships we faced.

I also learned to cherish the connections I had with others. A shared smile with a neighbor, a conversation with a friend, or an act of kindness from a stranger could lift my spirits in ways I had not anticipated. These interactions became lifelines, reinforcing the idea that, even in our struggles, we could find solace in one another.

The Essence of Hope

Through it all, I discovered that hope is not merely a distant dream but a tangible force that propels us forward. It is the flicker of light in the darkest moments, the belief that tomorrow holds the potential for change. Hope manifested itself in various forms—through the determination of my brothers to pursue their dreams, through the resilience of our community, and through the shared understanding that we were not defined solely by our struggles.

In conversations with Mahmood and Samir, I often emphasized the importance of hope. I wanted them to understand that while life could be challenging, it was also filled with possibilities. I encouraged them to embrace their passions and to believe in themselves, even when the world seemed unkind. Our discussions often revolved around envisioning a better future, one where our collective dreams could flourish despite the scars of our past.

As I reflected on our journey, I realized that the cost of survival was not solely measured in economic terms; it was also about the resilience of the human spirit. It was about finding the strength to rise above adversity, to cling to hope even when it seemed elusive.

In the end, the essence of our experience in Kurdistan was one of survival interwoven with beauty, hope, and the indomitable strength of family. Despite the challenges, we learned to live fully, embracing each moment with gratitude and the understanding that even in the face of hardship, life continued to offer us gifts—small reminders of joy, connection, and the promise of a brighter tomorrow.

Chapter 14: A Message of Hope

Refusing to Give Up: The Power of Resilience

In a world filled with uncertainty and adversity, resilience became my guiding principle. From the earliest days of my childhood in Iraq, through the tumultuous experiences of war, loss, and economic hardship, I learned that the ability to rise after falling is not just a trait but a choice—a conscious decision to keep moving forward, no matter how daunting the path ahead may seem.

Resilience is more than enduring hardship; it is the unwavering spirit to seek light even in the darkest of times. Throughout my journey, I witnessed countless individuals embody this strength. My brothers, for example, faced their own battles—navigating their education amid the pressures of our family's circumstances. Yet, they never succumbed to despair. Instead, they embraced challenges as opportunities for growth, proving that resilience can manifest in the form of hope and determination. Each setback they faced became a stepping stone toward a brighter future.

In moments of despair, I often reminded myself of the words my father shared before he passed: "Life is not merely about the challenges we face; it's about how we respond to them." This lesson became a cornerstone of my own resilience. It taught me that while I could not control external circumstances, I could control my mindset. Choosing to refuse defeat allowed me to transform pain into purpose, leveraging my experiences to inspire myself and others.

Believing in a Better Tomorrow Despite the Odds

As I continued to navigate the complexities of life in Kurdistan, the belief in a better tomorrow became a beacon of hope. Despite the numerous obstacles that seemed insurmountable, I learned that optimism is not blind; it is a powerful tool that fuels resilience. It is the belief that change is possible and that our circumstances do not define us.

I often found inspiration in the stories of others who had overcome adversity. Whether it was a fellow student who persevered through financial struggles to achieve academic success or a family member who turned their passion into a thriving business despite economic constraints, these narratives reaffirmed my conviction that a better future was achievable.

Moreover, I sought to cultivate this belief within my own family. I encouraged my brothers to pursue their dreams fiercely, emphasizing that obstacles were not signs of failure but rather opportunities for growth. Together, we shared our aspirations, creating a vision of the future that was brighter than our present struggles. This collective belief in a better tomorrow became a source of strength for us all, uniting us in our commitment to overcome adversity.

Final Thoughts: Hope is a Choice, and Life is a Journey of Resilience

As I reflect on my journey thus far, I recognize that hope is not merely a passive feeling; it is an active choice that requires courage and determination. It is the unwavering belief that, despite the challenges we face, we can carve out our own paths and create meaningful lives. This choice to embrace hope has been transformative, guiding me through the darkest of times and illuminating the way forward.

Life, I've come to understand, is a journey filled with ups and downs. It is not a linear path but a complex tapestry woven from moments of joy, sorrow, triumph, and despair. Each thread represents a lesson learned, a battle fought, and a victory celebrated. Through it all, the power of resilience shines brightly, reminding us that we have the capacity to adapt, grow, and thrive.

In sharing my story, I hope to inspire others to recognize their own resilience. Each of us has the strength to face our challenges, and in doing so, we can emerge stronger and more determined. We must remember that while the journey may be fraught with difficulties, it is also rich with opportunities for growth, connection, and hope.

As I stand on the precipice of my future, I carry with me the lessons learned from my past. I remain committed to choosing hope every day, to nurturing resilience within myself and my loved ones, and to fostering a community where we can uplift one another in our journeys. Together, we can transform our struggles into stories of triumph, illuminating the path for those who come after us.

In the end, life is not just about survival; it is about thriving, finding joy in the journey, and embracing the promise of tomorrow. Hope is a choice we make each day, a guiding light that illuminates our path and reminds us that, no matter how difficult the journey, we can rise again and again, stronger and more determined than ever before.

Epilogue: Looking Forward

The Importance of Hope, Family, and Perseverance

As I reflect on the winding journey that has brought me to this point, I am filled with a profound sense of gratitude. Hope, family, and perseverance have been the pillars upon which I've built my life. Each of these elements has played a crucial role in shaping my identity and guiding my choices, helping me navigate the labyrinth of experiences that life has presented.

Hope has been my steadfast companion, a light illuminating the darkest corners of my existence. It has fueled my desire to overcome obstacles and strive for a better future, reminding me that even in the face of adversity, possibilities abound. Through the trials I faced, hope became a beacon that urged me to keep moving forward, instilling in me the belief that every setback is but a setup for a comeback.

Family, too, has been a cornerstone of my resilience. My brothers, aunts, and grandmother have provided unwavering support, offering both love and encouragement when I needed it most. The bonds we share are a source of strength, reminding me that I am never alone in my struggles. Our collective experiences have woven a tapestry of shared dreams and aspirations, fostering an environment where we uplift and inspire one another. It is through these familial connections that I find the motivation to pursue my dreams, knowing that my success is intertwined with theirs.

Perseverance has been the thread that binds my journey together, a relentless drive to keep pushing forward despite the challenges that arise. It is the willingness to embrace discomfort and face fears head-on, to rise again after every fall. This tenacity has been essential, allowing me to adapt to the ever-changing circumstances of life and remain steadfast in the pursuit of my goals. It has taught me that resilience is not just about enduring hardship but actively choosing to rise above it.

A Future Yet Unwritten: Pursuing Dreams and Opportunities

As I stand at the threshold of a future yet unwritten, I am filled with a sense of anticipation. The possibilities that lie ahead are vast and varied, and I am eager to embrace the opportunities that await me. The lessons learned from my past will serve as a guiding compass as I navigate this new chapter of my life.

With each passing day, I am reminded that dreams are not static; they evolve and transform as we grow. I hold within me a myriad of aspirations—some rooted in my experiences in the field of petroleum engineering, others ignited by newfound passions that have emerged along the way. I envision a future where I can contribute meaningfully to my community, where I can harness my skills and knowledge to make a positive impact in the world.

I remain committed to lifelong learning, understanding that education does not end with a degree but continues throughout life. Whether through further studies, workshops, or simply engaging with diverse perspectives, I am dedicated to expanding my horizons and refining my craft. I aim to channel my experiences into mentorship, guiding others who may find themselves on similar paths, sharing the wisdom I have gleaned from my journey.

Moreover, I aspire to foster connections that transcend borders and cultures. In our increasingly interconnected world, the sharing of ideas and experiences has the power to break down barriers and create a more inclusive society. I hope to engage with individuals from various backgrounds, learning from their stories and contributing my own. Together, we can inspire one another to dream bigger and reach higher, uniting in our shared humanity.

As I look to the future, I am filled with a sense of responsibility—not only to myself but to those who have supported me along the way. I strive to honor the sacrifices made by my family and the lessons instilled in me by my upbringing. It is my hope that, by pursuing my dreams and embracing new opportunities, I can contribute to a legacy of resilience and hope for generations to come.

In closing, the journey of life is a tapestry woven with threads of hope, family, and perseverance. While the past has shaped who I am today, it is the future that excites me the most. With an open heart and a determined spirit, I am ready to embrace whatever lies ahead, confident that the story of my life is far from over. Each day is a blank page, an opportunity to write new chapters filled with adventure, growth, and boundless possibilities.

Acknowledgement

As I pen these words, I am overwhelmed with gratitude for the many individuals who have shaped my journey and supported me through the trials and triumphs of life. This book is as much a reflection of their love and encouragement as it is of my own experiences.

First and foremost, I extend my deepest thanks to my beloved brothers. Your unwavering support, strength, and camaraderie have been my anchor through the storms. Together, we have navigated the darkest valleys and celebrated the brightest peaks. I am proud to walk this path with you.

To my relatives, who have always been a source of love and guidance, your faith in me has inspired me to reach for my dreams, even when the odds seemed insurmountable. Your sacrifices and shared memories remind me of the strength of our family bonds.

I would also like to express my heartfelt appreciation to my friends, especially those who stood by me during my most challenging moments. Your kindness, laughter, and encouragement have been a lifeline, reminding me that I am never alone on this journey. Each shared story and heartfelt conversation has enriched my life and given me the courage to persevere.

A special acknowledgment goes to my mentors and educators, who ignited my passion for learning and instilled in me the belief that knowledge is a powerful tool for transformation. Your dedication to nurturing my potential has made a lasting impact on my life.

Finally, I thank my readers for taking the time to delve into my story. I hope that by sharing my experiences, I can inspire others to find strength in their struggles, cherish their loved ones, and pursue their dreams with unwavering determination.

With all my love and gratitude,

Acknowledgment of AI Assistance

In crafting this memoir, I have drawn deeply from my personal experiences, reflections, and insights. However, I also embraced the capabilities of artificial intelligence to enhance my writing process.

While the heart and soul of this narrative are rooted in my life, I utilized AI tools to assist in generating outlines and expanding upon my ideas. This collaboration allowed me to structure my thoughts more effectively and articulate my journey with clarity and depth.

I believe that the fusion of human creativity and technological assistance can lead to unique storytelling possibilities. By leveraging AI, I aimed to create a richer reading experience that resonates with authenticity while embracing modern innovation.

Thank you for joining me on this journey. I hope you find inspiration in my story as much as I found in the process of bringing it to life.